WE CAN DRAW
CATS

Corina Jeffries

WINDMILL
BOOKS

New York

Published in 2023 by Windmill Books, an Imprint of Rosen Publishing
29 East 21st Street, New York, NY 10010

Portions of this work were originally authored by Laura Murawski and published as *How to Draw Cats*. All new material this edition authored by Corina Jeffries.

Library of Congress Cataloging-in-Publication Data
Names: Jeffries, Corina, author.
Title: We can draw cats / Corina Jeffries.
Description: New York : Windmill Books, [2023] | Series: We can draw |
   Includes index. | Audience: Grades 2-3
Identifiers: LCCN 2021057032 (print) | LCCN 2021057033 (ebook) | ISBN
   9781508198062 (library binding) | ISBN 9781508198048 (paperback) | ISBN
   9781508198055 (set) | ISBN 9781508198079 (ebook)
Subjects: LCSH: Cats in art–Juvenile literature. |
   Drawing–Technique–Juvenile literature.
Classification: LCC NC783.8.C36 J44 2023 (print) | LCC NC783.8.C36
   (ebook) | DDC 743.6/9752–dc23/eng/20220111
LC record available at https://lccn.loc.gov/2021057032
LC ebook record available at https://lccn.loc.gov/2021057033

Designer: Leslie Taylor
Editor: Caitie McAneney

Photo credits: Cover, p. 1 (cat) Karen-Richards/Shutterstock.com; series artwork (pencils) suriya yapin/Shutterstock.com; series artwork (art table) insta_photos/Shutterstock.com; series artwork (banner) Kathy Kiselova/Shutterstock.com; series artwork (scribbles) mart/Shutterstock.com; pp. 4, 10 Nynke van Holten/Shutterstock.com; p. 5 (pencils) ILLUSTOR STUDIO/Shutterstock.com; p. 5 (girl) Ruslan Huzau/Shutterstock.com; p. 6 WilleeCole Photography/Shuttertstock.com; p. 8 Ermolaev Alexander/Shutterstock.com; p. 12 Juniors Bildarchiv GmbH/Alamy Stock Photo; p. 14 chrisbrignell/Shutterstock.com; p. 16 Valentyna Chukhlyebova/Shutterstock.com; p. 18 totophotos/Shutterstock.com; p. 20 ZUMA Press, Inc./Alamy Stock Photo.

Manufactured in the United States of America

CPSIA compliance information: Batch #CSWM23: For further information contact Rosen Publishing, New York, New York at 1-800-237-9932.

Find us on

CONTENTS

CRAZY FOR CATS

Cats are some of the most popular pets in the world. They've been popular pets throughout history. In fact, scientists believe that cats were kept as pets as far back as 9,500 years ago. They're cute. They're cuddly. They're also often helpful for **rodent** control, especially on farms.

This book will teach you how to draw eight different kinds of cats, from ancient cats to today's domestic cats. Domestic, or household, **breeds** are very different from one another. Longhaired cats may have come from the Asian wildcat. Shorthaired cats are believed to have come from a species, or kind, of African wildcat. Grab your drawing supplies, and get ready to learn more about cats!

What kinds of cats do you want to draw? This book will first introduce you to kittens and Halloween cats. Next, you'll learn about different domestic breeds. Then, you'll learn about cats throughout history. The more you know about a certain kind of cat, the more interesting they are to draw!

Gather your drawing materials!

You'll need a pencil, pencil sharpener, eraser, and paper. You might want to make your drawings in a sketch pad.

CUTE KITTENS!

Kittens are full of playful energy. They love to jump, swat, run, chase, and hide. While we see this as playing, there's actually a reason behind their actions. This is how they practice their hunting skills! Kittens usually learn these skills by the time they are nine weeks old. Kittens are able to hunt like adult cats by the time they are 12 weeks old.

The kitten you will draw is practicing a skill called the "bird swat." This involves jumping into the air and swatting at their **prey**. To practice their "fish scoop," a kitten makes a flipping motion as its claws get ready to toss a fish out of water. To practice their "mouse pounce," a kitten will leap into the air and spring down on a toy or other cat.

Some behaviors are natural to kittens, but many hunting skills are learned from their mothers.

1

To begin, draw a long oval. Then, draw two circles at the top and bottom that cross the oval.

2

For the arms, draw two pairs of curved lines. One pair goes up from the oval and one goes down.

3

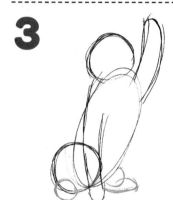

At the bottom of the oval, draw two little circles. Add a curved shape to make the kitten's back paw.

4

For the ears, draw triangle shapes on the head. For the tail, add a C shape on the left side of the circle.

5

Now, shape the kitten's back by adding lines as shown in the illustration. Also, curve the lines of the front legs and paws. Add a little ball of yarn to the top right side of the drawing as if the cat is batting at it.

6

Make a small triangle for the nose, two small ovals for the eyes, and lines for the mouth. Add lines for the toes.

7

Finish the paws, eyes, and nose. Add lines in the ears and on the face for whiskers. Shade the body as shown. Erase any extra lines. Your cute kitten is all done!

SCARY CATS!

From decorations to costumes, black cats go hand in hand with Halloween. Sometimes Halloween cats are shown with their backs arched, as if they're angry and about to attack. These cats are often hissing, with their teeth sharp and scary.

Throughout history, black cats have been a **symbol** of bad luck. This is because in many societies, the color black is connected to death and illness. Most likely, **myths** about black cats originally came from Europe in the **Middle Ages**. It was believed that witches would sometimes take the shape of a black cat. Today, we know black cats aren't evil or dangerous. They're just a different color!

Black cats and pumpkins are common symbols of Halloween.

1

First, draw three circles of different sizes. Look to the illustration to see how they should cross each other.

2

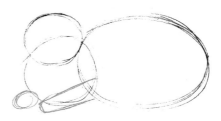

At the bottom of the middle circle, draw a tiny circle and a rectangular shape. You just made the front leg and paws.

3

Next, draw the ears at the top of the upper circle. Add two curved lines to the larger circle for the tail. Draw a "t" in the face to act as a guide for the next steps.

4

Join the head to the body by making a curve as seen here. Curve the lines for the front paw and leg. Using the "t" guide, add the eyes and nose.

5

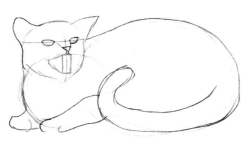

Add details to the face and paws as shown here. To draw an opened mouth, make a vertical rectangle below the nose. Add a triangle to the left of the rectangle.

6

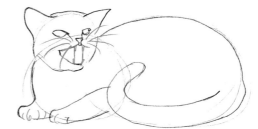

Make four pointed shapes at each corner of the rectangle for the teeth. Add curved lines for the whiskers near the nose. Draw curved lines on the paws to make the toes.

7

Erase any extra lines. Shade in the mouth, the eyes, and the nose. You can even shade in the fur to make the cat all black.

MEET THE SIAMESE CAT

Many different breeds of cats exist in the world. The Siamese cat often has a long, lean body, beautiful fur, and bright blue eyes. Its small head is shaped like a wedge, almost like a triangle, and its eyes slant towards its nose. It has a long, skinny tail. It's often a great jumper. The Siamese cat is known to have a very loud voice and to make a lot of noise.

A Siamese cat is born nearly all white or cream-colored. As it gets older, it gets darker shades of color on certain areas of its body, such as its face. The temperature of the place where it is raised affects fur color. The warmer the temperature, the lighter its fur will be. Siamese cats originally came from Thailand, a Southeast Asian country that used to be called Siam.

Many Siamese cats have blue eyes. Unfortunately, they often have poor vision.

1

Start by drawing two small ovals and one bigger oval. Look to the illustration to note how one of the small ovals crosses the bigger oval.

2

Use three lines to connect the ovals.

3

Now draw a tall, curved shape from the top left of the biggest oval for the tail.

4

Make two angular shapes beneath the biggest oval for the back legs as shown here.

5

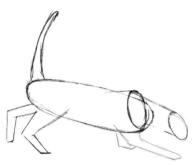

Make two more angular shapes at the other end of the big oval for the front legs.

6

For the ears, draw two triangles with rounded tops at the top of the small oval on the right. Add a "t" to the face to act as a guide for the next step.

7

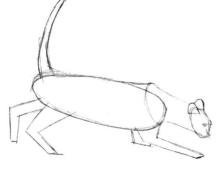

Using the "t" guide, draw an eye, nose, and mouth.

8

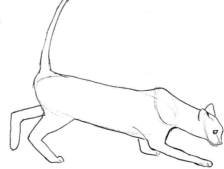

Curve the lines. Erase any extra lines. You've just drawn a special Siamese cat!

MEET THE MANX CAT

The Manx cat comes from the Isle of Man, an island off the northwest coast of England. Some Manx cats are born without tails, while some have stumps. Scientists think this happens because of a **genetic mutation**. A Manx cat with no tail is called a "rumpy." A cat with a small bump under the skin is called a "rumpy riser." A short-tailed Manx is a "stumpy" or "stubby," while one with a longer tail is a "longy."

The gorilla Koko, who is famous for learning sign language, is a big fan of Manx cats. She kept several of them as pets. Manx cats have large, round heads and eyes. They have very thick fur, which keeps them warm in colder temperatures. Manx cats love to play and jump, and they are great hunters.

Manx cats have back legs that are longer than their front legs. This causes the Manx to hop like a rabbit.

1

To start, draw two circles and one small oval. Place them according to the illustration provided.

2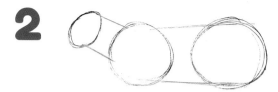

Next, draw four lines to connect the circles.

3

Add two angular shapes below the middle circle for the front legs.

4

Add two more angular shapes below the circle to the right for the back legs.

5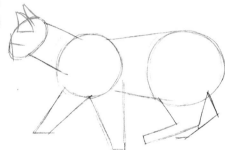

Add two triangular shapes to the small oval to make the ears. Add a "t" to the front to act as a guide for the next step.

6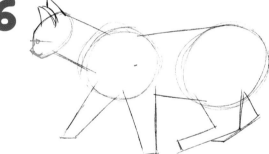

Using the "t" guide, draw an eye, nose, and mouth.

7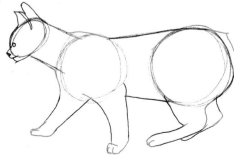

Add a tiny bump where a tail would be. Connect and curve the lines in your drawing to shape the body and paws.

8

Shade in the striped pattern of the fur, which is common for the Manx. Erase your extra lines. You've drawn a magnificent Manx cat!

SPHYNX CATS

You may have heard of the sphinx in ancient Greek myths. It's a winged monster with a lion's body and a woman's head. Ancient Egyptians also built a structure called the Great Sphinx near the Pyramids of Giza. The Sphynx, however, isn't a mythical creature—it's a breed of modern cat!

The first Sphynx was born in 1966 in Toronto, Canada. Originally called Canadian hairless cats, Sphynxes were supposedly named after the Great Sphinx in Egypt. It's a cat with very little hair, or fur. The cat's coat, or fur covering, is fine and short, like peach fuzz. Hairlessness is a genetic mutation. People bred cats to create this new hairless breed.

Sphynx cats have very large, upright ears and large eyes set far apart on the face. Their loose skin looks wrinkled.

1

First, draw two ovals, one large and one small. Look to the illustration for their placement.

2

Next, connect the two ovals with two curved lines.

3

Draw two sets of curved lines from the large oval to make the front legs. Join each pair of lines with a straight line at the bottom.

4

Add two angular shapes at the bottom of the large oval, as shown, to make the back legs.

5

Draw two curved lies and join them to make the tail. Add two triangles at the top for ears. Add lines as guides for the nose and eyes.

6

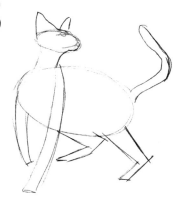

Draw the face. Add an oval shape for an eye. Draw a tiny upside-down triangle for the nose and a line for the mouth.

7

Two lines down from the face as shown here. Add curved lines to make the paws. Curve the lines of the legs.

8

Erase extra lines in your drawing. Then, shade in your cat. Sphynxes can have multiple colors and patterns on their skin. You've finished your Sphynx cat!

15

FIERCE FANGS!

A million years ago, the saber-toothed cat was a fierce predator. These huge cats were named for two long, curved, sharp teeth that grew out of their upper jaw. A saber-toothed cat's teeth could grow to about 8 inches (20.3 cm) long. They used these teeth, called fangs, to bite through the flesh of their prey. In what is now North America, saber-toothed cats probably hunted bison and **mastodons**.

Most scientists believe that large saber-toothed cats walked flat-footed, like bears—unlike today's domestic cats that walk on their toes. Saber-toothed cats died out about 11,700 years ago from **climate change**, human contact, or loss of prey. We study them now through **fossils** they left behind.

This shows what the saber-toothed cat may have looked like. These cats existed from around 56 million to 11,700 years ago.

1

To start, draw a large oval for the body. To make the head, add a smaller oval to the left. Draw it crossing the first oval.

2

Now draw two rectangular shapes beneath the body. Notice how one rectangular shape goes away from the body at an angle.

3

For the other legs, draw two angular shapes behind the rectangular shapes.

4

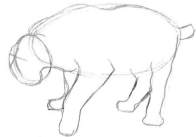

To shape the back, draw curved lines at the top of the large oval. For the tail, draw a "U" on its side. Add curved lines to the legs and head. Draw a "t" inside of the head to help draw the face.

5

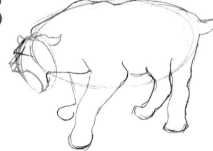

Using the "t" guide, draw the head, ears, nose, and open mouth. Notice how the nose looks like a tiny triangle and the mouth looks like a backward "C."

6

Draw another backward "C" inside the one you already have. Connect the two "C" shapes with a line. For the two front teeth, add two curved, pointed shapes.

7

Lastly, add a semicircle for an eye, curved lines for whiskers, and curved lines in the paws for the toes. Erase any extra lines. That's one fierce saber-toothed cat!

CATS IN ANCIENT EGYPT

Cats were very important animals in ancient Egypt. They were seen as magical creatures that brought good luck. They were sometimes even dressed in jewels. The Egyptian goddess Bastet was portrayed as a cat or a woman with a cat's head. She was thought to have special powers. Bastet protected babies, children, and birthing mothers.

The Egyptians built a temple in honor of Bastet. People who came to **worship** at the temple brought **mummified** cats to bury nearby. These dead cats had been treated with special chemicals to keep them from rotting. Egyptians also wore small figures of cats on necklaces or made cat statues to protect them from evil. These mummified cats and **artifacts** teach us a lot about cats in ancient Egypt.

Shown here is an Egyptian cat statue. Follow the steps on the next page to draw Bastet!

1

To form the body of Bastet, first draw two circles. Then draw a large oval that crosses the bottom circle. Notice where the different shapes are placed.

2

To form the front legs, draw three straight lines down from the middle circle.

3

To make the cat's face, start by drawing part of a rectangle coming out of the top circle, as shown in the illustration. Draw an angular shape at the bottom of the three leg lines. This will make paws. Add another part of a rectangle at the bottom of the large oval.

4

To make the front of the neck, the front paws, and the back paws, draw curved lines. To make the back of the neck, add a straight line to join the first and second circles.

5

Next, add ears to the top circle. Curve the lines at the front of the face. Add a small curved line to the back of the shoulders. Add two curved lines at the bottom of the drawing for the tail.

6

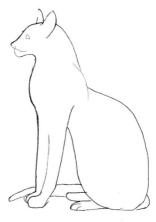

Now draw an eye, the mouth, and the nose. Add lines in the paws for the toes. Erase any extra lines. Your drawing of Bastet will likely look like this!

A TV STAR

Some cats have become famous for playing parts on TV and in movies. For example, Morris was the name of a cat in commercials for 9Lives Cat Food. He was known as the "world's most **finicky** cat," and he would only eat this kind of cat food. He became so popular with TV viewers that he even appeared on talk shows! Morris was also listed as the author of several books about cats.

Morris has always been an American shorthaired tabby with orange fur. The first Morris was rescued from an animal shelter near Chicago, Illinois, in 1968. Over the years, other rescue cats played Morris. In 2006, Morris's Million Cat Rescue tried to find homes for cats.

Between 1969 and 1978, Morris was part of 58 commercials. He won the PATSY—which is like an Oscar for animals—in 1972 and 1973.

1

To begin drawing Morris, draw three circles. Make them larger in size from the top to the bottom. The two larger circles should cross each other.

2

Now, join the small and medium circles by drawing two lines. Add two angular shapes, as shown, to make the front legs.

3

Draw two shapes, as shown, on the bottom of the large circle to make the back legs. Draw an oval to make the tail, and connect it to the large circle with a curved line.

4

Make a curved line to join the medium and large circles. Add rounded triangles for ears on top of the small circle. Draw two lines in the shape of a "t" to serve as a guide for the face. Add a line to one paw as shown.

5

Using the "t" lines as a guide, draw the eyes, the nose, and the tongue. To make the shoulders, draw a curved line between the rear ear and the middle circle.

6

Add a few curved lines for the whiskers. Draw four small circles around a larger circle on the paw of the raised leg for the paw pads. Add curved lines for the toes and smaller ones for the claws.

7

Erase any extra lines. Now, shade in your drawing according to the striped pattern of Morris's fur. By controlling the direction of shading around his body, you can create the feeling of fur. Your picture of Morris shows him licking his paw to clean himself!

GLOSSARY

artifact: Something made by humans in the past that still exists.

breed: A group of animals that share features different from other groups of the kind.

climate change: Change in Earth's weather caused by human activity.

finicky: Very hard to please; fussy.

fossil: The marks or remains of plants and animals that formed over thousands or millions of years.

genetic mutation: A difference from the norm in an animal's genes, or the matter that determines how the body looks and acts.

mastodon: A type of extinct animal from the elephant family.

Middle Ages: The period of European history from about 500 CE to about 1500 CE.

mummify: To make into a mummy.

myth: A story, often involving superhuman beings, that attempts to describe the origin of a people's customs or beliefs, or explain mysterious events.

prey: An animal hunted by other animals for food.

rodent: A small, furry animal with large front teeth, such as a mouse or rat.

symbol: Something that stands for something else.

worship: To honor a god or gods.

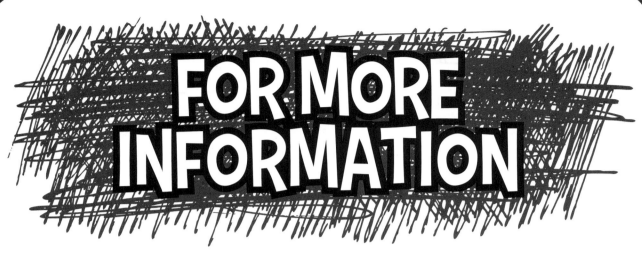

FOR MORE INFORMATION

WEBSITES

Smilodon

www.dkfindout.com/us/dinosaurs-and-prehistoric-life/prehistoric-mammals/smilodon/#!
Learn more about Smilodon, one of the ancient species of saber-toothed cats.

Cats Rule in Ancient Egypt

kids.nationalgeographic.com/pages/article/cats-rule-in-ancient-egypt
Discover how ancient Egyptians honored their cats at this website.

BOOKS

Lynch, Seth. *Cats Close Up*. New York, NY: Gareth Stevens Publishing, 2023.

Rober, Harold T. *Saber-Toothed Cat*. Minneapolis, MN: Lerner Publications, 2017.

INDEX